DESIGN IN
BLACK & WHITE

a black silk ballgown with white tulle underlay • a Christian Dior suit in a Philippe Starck-

a Robert Doisneau photograph on a white gallery wall • Audrey Hepburn in My Fair Lady • a page designed bedroom • a Mies van der Rohe Barcelona chair on a black-and-white checkered floor •

of print • Cecil Beatonesque stripes • Anouska Hempel's hotels • the very essence of style

Maxalto Amoenus Ottoman
Photography courtesy of Space Furniture, Australia.

DESIGN IN
BLACK & WHITE

Janelle McCulloch

Principal photography by Janelle McCulloch

Published in Australia in 2010 by
The Images Publishing Group Pty Ltd
ABN 89 059 734 431
6 Bastow Place, Mulgrave, Victoria 3170, Australia
Tel: +61 3 9561 5544 Fax: +61 3 9561 4860
books@imagespublishing.com
www.imagespublishing.com

Copyright © The Images Publishing Group Pty Ltd 2010
The Images Publishing Group Reference Number: 867

National Library of Australia Cataloguing-in-Publication entry:

Author:	McCulloch, Janelle
Title:	Design in black & white / Janelle McCulloch.
ISBN:	9781864702910 (hbk.)
Subjects:	Black.
	White.
	Color in design.
Dewey Number:	701.85

Coordinating editor: Andrew Hall

Designed by The Graphic Image Studio Pty Ltd, Mulgrave, Australia
www.tgis.com.au

Pre-publishing services by SC (Sang Choy) International Pte Ltd, Singapore

Printed on 140 gsm Chinese Matt Art paper by Paramount Printing Company Limited, Hong Kong

IMAGES has included on its website a page for special notices in relation to this and our other publications. Please visit www.imagespublishing.com.

CONTENTS

INTRODUCTION

Glamour and Grandeur

The combination of black and white has always been dramatic. The traditional shades of high society and refined design, these two classic tones have represented inimitable luxury and unparalleled glamour since the early 20th century. Think of black and white and you think of a well-tailored tuxedo with a crisp white dress shirt or a little black dress with a perfect string of pearls; of a smartly striped summer marquee and a misty-eyed bride and groom in a long white gown and a debonair black suit; of a midnight-colored Aston Martin with cream leather seats or a white Parisian apartment with glossy black floorboards and a beautifully styled salon. It's a combination that's bold, highly stylized and memorably glamorous. And it never seems to date, no matter how many other colors and shades bypass it in the ever-changing fashion stakes. It's no wonder many designers believe that black and white represent sophistication at its best, elegance at its most alluring.

Of the many great 20th-century designers who have recognized the power of black and white, Coco Chanel and Christian Dior were among the first to achieve international fame for their dramatic treatment of these two powerful contrasts. Dior secured his reputation by draping white satin bows over a long black velvet dress and creating heart-stopping silhouettes out of decadent yards of ivory shantung and dark gray taffeta. He also made the elegant houndstooth check one of his signature motifs, using it on everything from neo-Louis XVI chairs to perfume bottles. Chanel, meanwhile, so adored the effect of black on white (and white on black) she designed many of her collections as an ode to monochromatic glamour, and then created the ultimate tribute: a timeless, perfectly simple perfume bottle with a perfectly effortless black and white label that she called, quite simply, No. 5.

Black and white also came to be valued by architects and furniture designers, particularly Modernists such as Mies van der Rohe, Le Corbusier, Alvar Aalto, Charles and Ray Eames, Arne Jacobsen, Isamu Noguchi, Richard Neutra, Eero Saarinen, Hans Wegner, and Rudolf Schindler, among many others. Already advocates of the simplicity of line and clarity of form, these designers, particularly those of the mid-century era, embraced the beauty of black and its elegant opposite white, and produced everything from buildings to furniture pieces inspired by the two minimalist tones.

Adopting Henry Ford's philosophy of using any color as long as it was black—or white—many of these iconic designers produced eye-catching pieces that are still considered classics today. Think of Mies van der Rohe's Barcelona daybed and Brno chair and Le Corbusier's chaise longue, their sleek black forms representing the ultimate in sophisticated furniture design. After the mid-century, many Modernist homes even became white as clutter was eschewed in favor of simple, clean, pared-back architectural forms and spaces. These almost monastic interiors also served as the perfect backdrop for the sophisticated furniture pieces that filled these rooms, most of them dressed in black. It was a cool, minimalist feel that looked to Mies van der Rohe and the International Style for inspiration, but also beat its own quiet drum.

Later, architects such as Richard Meier built on the look of classic Modern architecture by designing white buildings so glamorous they immediately become iconic and turned their creator into something of a celebrity. Others, including designers Andrée Putman, Anouska Hempel, Christian Liaigre, Frédéric Méchiche, Catherine Memmi, Giorgio Armani, and John Pawson, fused black and white together in such a way that the interiors they created were so coolly beautiful they eventually helped the monochrome look to become one of the defining signature styles of the minimalist 1990s. As Armani explained, they represented "simplicity and purity." For purists, black and white were indeed the most perfect shades around.

Now, after a few years of being overshadowed by beiges, grays, and a vast palette of other dizzyingly chic colors, black and white are being revived again as increasing numbers of aesthetes realize just how eye-catching these impeccable tones can be. Whether understated or glamorously Hollywood in style, black and white continue to be two of the most beautiful shades in the language of design.

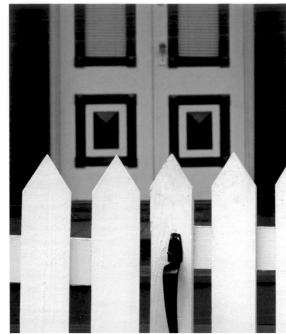

Beautiful black-and-white houses in the Old Town part of Key West, a fascinating island at the very end of the Florida Keys. Despite the proximity to the Caribbean, most of the homes in this gracious part of town are architectural odes to monochrome. Opposite: A typical porch.

A Modern Interpretation of the Classic Design Duet
Black and White in the 21st Century

Theories vary as to why the classic combination of black and white has once again become the height of chic. It may be that we have entered a more tasteful age, having learned a few decorating lessons from the riotous shades of the previous few decades, or it may simply be that monochrome tones increasingly suit our streamlined lifestyles—offering us clarity and balance while the world around us becomes more frenetic and kaleidoscopic in pace and shade. Whatever the reason, there is no doubt that black and white have come to the forefront of 21st-century design. Sexy, edgy, sharply sophisticated and minimalist in a way that feels harmonious and composed rather than uncomfortably austere, black and white are the defining shades of the new millennium. On their own they represent elegance at the opposite ends of the decorating spectrum. Together, they signify perfect order and inimitable style.

One of the most noticeable places where black and white has had a dramatic re-entrance is the gilt-edged fantasyland known as Tinsel Town, where—much like a star being reborn—the design duet seems to be experiencing a decorating comeback. Inspired by classic designers such as William Haines and Dorothy Draper, who both had a flair for the dramatic (and as such were loved by Hollywood's elite), the decorators and designers of Los Angeles are drawing upon black and white to give their rooms an injection of old-fashioned glamour. And the new look certainly mirrors the cool elegance of 1920s, 30s, and 40s films. Glimmering crystal chandeliers, Venetian glass mirrors, high-gloss black lacquer armoires and side tables, Art Deco pieces, mirrored dressing tables, sculptured cream carpets, and a color palette that never strays far from black, white, vanilla, taupe, and ice blue work together like a carefully choreographed movie set to create—or recreate—a new design style.

Big on detail—and cinematic drama—and small on subtlety, the New Hollywood look has made decorating headlines in recent years as it takes the design world by storm. Leading interior designer Kelly Wearstler, who was one of the first to look to the past for modern inspiration, leaned heavily on the Hollywood Regency look when it came to decorating the Viceroy hotels in Santa Monica and Palm Springs, while legendary American fashion designer Ralph Lauren recalled the look of classic films and movie stars for several of his most recent homewares collections, including Modern Hollywood and Bel Air.

As the marketing spiel for Bel Air reads: "The blithe pattern play of black and white brings drama to soigné settings that recall the impeccably tailored glamour of 1940s films. Crisp houndstooth checks, elegant pinstripes, and fanciful detailing complement piano black furnishings …" Looking at Lauren's collection, it's easy to see why they've been so popular. The precise lines, graceful shapes, and shimmering surfaces enhance the already refined style of the creamy white and black lacquer pieces, including cocktail cabinets, side tables, simple sofas, and chaise longues, lending a movie-star air to spaces. It is certainly Hollywood glamour, redefined with modern clarity for a new generation of aesthetes in search of a new kind of elegance.

However, it isn't just Hollywood where black and white have been spotted by the design paparazzi. The world's fashion catwalks have recently witnessed a black-and-white blitz as fashion designers rediscover the fabulousness of this dignified duet. Ralph Lauren, Giorgio Armani, Carolina Herrera, Jean Paul Gaultier, Stella McCartney, Oscar de la Renta, and Karl Lagerfeld designing for Chanel have all drawn on the drama of

monochromatic decadence for their recent collections, invoking the great names of Chanel and Dior as they've done so. This "re-enacting of the classics," as many fashion editors put it, was so well received by the fashion and design worlds that all the black-and-white detailing has started to influence the home, inspiring decorators to copy the couture looks off the catwalk as well—often quite literally. Lifestyle magazines are now full of luxury homes and apartments featuring graphic houndstooth patterns, glamorous on armchairs; traffic-stopping zebra prints, startlingly beautiful on ottomans; smartly buttoned white sofas, exquisitely matched with black-buttoned cushions; black-and-white striped wallpaper, gorgeous in libraries and halls; and other immaculately tailored interior spaces.

Ebony furniture has become the little-black-dress equivalent—transforming a room with an instantly chic lift—while some designers have gone all way and outfitted entire rooms in midnight shades, claiming it has the same impressive effect as it does with clothing. In places such as Manhattan, interior designers have begun to take their aesthetic cues straight from the famous tailoring district of London's Savile Row, adopting the

pinstripes, chalkstripes, white cuffs, windowpane checks, and other suiting elements of traditional gentlemen's outfits to create witty and whimsical interiors designed for fussy clients who want interiors with finesse. Of course, these are clearly interiors designed for the limousine lifestyle—spaces are dressed as if black-and-white soirées happened regularly and tuxedos and pearls are often seen cavorting among the furniture—but even so, the "banker stripe" look has been so effective it's now gaining popularity with those who have neither a housekeeper or butler to call their own. Even inexpensive bedding is now often laced with tuxedo pleats or fine black piping. It's a little bit of penthouse to add punch to your studio apartment.

And in hotels, too, black and white are making their mark, most noticeably in the new design hotels that are popping up in the most stylish corners of the globe. Boston, London, Manhattan, and Mexico are just some of the places where monochromatic palettes have been used to jazz up hotel spaces, and the international jetsetters are embracing the glamorous graphics with relish.

Modern Classics, New Minimalism, Luxe Redux. Call it what you will, but there is no doubt that black and white have stormed back into fashion. It's a firm return to glamour and it's bringing sophistication back into the home. As Edward M. Tashjian, vice-president of marketing for America's Century Furniture, said: "In a world where things are getting muddier, people are looking for absolutes. [Black and white] represent balance, the yin and the yang."

White
A State of Grace

The Taj Mahal, the White House, a John Pawson-designed home, a cliff-top property in Santorini, a Barcelona daybed by Mies van der Rohe, a Fritz Hansen Egg chair by Arne Jacobsen, a mother-of-pearl jewelry case, a Hollywood gown, a string of pearls, a vintage claw-footed bath in a white-tiled bathroom, Ursula Andress rising out of the sea in a clinging white bikini, crisp Egyptian cotton bed linen, fine porcelain dinner ware, an Apple MacBook, a feather, a shell, a spring lamb, the white garden at Sissinghurst, the all-white suite at The Hempel hotel in London, a waffle cone full of dripping vanilla ice cream, a tub full of piping-hot popcorn, sundresses, shop awnings, business shirts, sandshoes, slipcover sofas in white-timber beach houses, a white linen shirt with a well-worn pair of jeans, a tiny rowboat at the end of a painted pier, a vase full of Easter lilies to celebrate living.

White is the color world's quietest shade. Understated, elegant, delicate, and diplomatic (it relates beautifully to every color), it is the opposite of dramatic, theatrical black in so many ways. In fact, it is so calm and quiet that there is a danger of overlooking it in favor of bolder, more vibrant shades.

To do so, however, would be a design mistake, as white has just as much depth and character as its louder, look-at-me cousins on the color wheel—and just as much power to produce the wow factor. Think of classic Greek architecture or the Taj Mahal or the White Garden at Sissinghurst Castle in England. White allows the grace and shape of a building or structure—whether horticultural or architectural—to show through. Indeed, such is its ability to distill form down to its essence while showing off design's fine lines that the "white-on-white" combination has become one of the most popular styles in modern interiors. Full of beauty and simplicity, white truly is elegance at its most alluring.

While white can be breathtaking in its simplicity, it can also exhibit a surprisingly versatile, chameleon-like personality. It can be traditional or modern, timeless or edgy, romantic or dramatic, high-glam or low-key. It can be luminous and fresh, or gently worn and endearingly rustic—think of the well-aged white of a beach house or boat shed. It can be succinct or it can be complicated, and it can be sporty—think of polo, cricket, or a white convertible on an open coast road—or it can be reflective—white gardens, white galleries, nuns wearing white habits in an all-white convent.

White can be a symbol of serenity, a state of grace, or a reflection of elegance. Or it can be a showstopper like no other—think of Marilyn Monroe's dresses or First Lady Michelle Obama's inauguration gown or a cute white sundress, which, when worn with a pair of heels and a tan, can stop traffic on a hot summer's day. No wonder when many people want to make an entrance—such as brides, for example, who don't just wear it because it reflects purity and glamour in equal measure—they usually choose white.

Gracious, stylish, sophisticated, and timeless, white has many sides to it. But whatever tone, trait, or characteristic it takes on, there is no doubt about it: it's always sublime.

Symbolic connotations attached to white

Simplicity, purity, innocence, cleanliness, hope, peace, humility

White paint by any other name

Macaroon, Milk and Honey, Modesty, Oyster, Old Church White, Ecru, Pannacotta, Parchment, White Truffle, White With Wine Glass Bay, Napkin, Whisper, Cord, Cottontail, China, Colorado, Barrister, Antique, Bianca, Berkshire, Jodhpurs, White Knight, White Tie, Smoke, Sea Foam, Seattle, Marilyn's Dress, Picket Fence, Winter's Day, Whitewash, Sailor's Knot, Key Largo Road, Montauk Driftwood, Nantucket Garden, Miami Bright, Old Verandah, Vintage Roadster, Polo Mallett, Writer's Journal, Art Gallery, Ageless

"Style is ... Charleston in South Carolina, Givenchy, the Paris Opera House, white, Margot Fonteyn, any Cole Porter song, and English pageantry ..."

Noel Coward

Black
A Statement of Style and Sophistication

A London cab, a tuxedo on the town, a glossy front door on a beautiful house, a pair of just-shined shoes, a sexy dress, a black-clad Italian in a brand new Ferrari, a pair of oversized Jackie O-style glasses (best worn with an oh-so-cute LBD), a cobble-stoned road in a city after a deluge of spring rain, a dog's nose, the night sky (even blacker in the country), a sweep of mascara on a Hollywood star, a string of black pearls, a black kitten, a black gown at a black-tie ball, a blackboard menu in a Parisian café, a black Labrador greeting a black French poodle on a white gravel garden path, a black staircase winding up from a black-and-white checkerboard hall, an onyx ring, a pinstripe suit on an ambitious young banker, a black thoroughbred, a black Rolls Royce, a little black book full of favorite names, a bar of the richest dark chocolate, a set of lacy lingerie, a black alligator handbag, a sleek black phone, a black polo neck sweater on a cheeky Irish poet, a beautiful hatbox tied with a big black bow, the color of style, the color of luxury.

Much has been written about black over the years. It's a shade that tends to attract attention, in good ways and bad. Indeed, few other colors have the ability to polarize people as much as black. You could say it is the color world's most controversial—and misunderstood—hue.

For the creative and aesthetic set, black is, and will always be, "the new black." For these aesthetes, it is timelessly beautiful and far from dull; a shade that reflects depth, style, elegance, and of course that famous high-voltage glamour, whether it's used in lingerie or limousines. Fashion designers delight in using black in their collections because it's seen by many of them as the epitome of sophistication. Architects adore wearing it in their studios and workspaces, perhaps because it represents an ideal blank canvas upon which to work their architectural talents. Graphic designers and publishers favor black's dark lines because it shows creative articulation and liquid grace. Industrial designers—including car, camera, pen, laptop, and mobile phone designers—usually use black because it lends itself to modern design, reflecting luxury and refinement in ways that few colors do. And business professionals turn to it time and time again when planning their professional wardrobes because it shows dignity, credibility, intelligence, and quiet style in equal measures.

Others, however, are less enamored of this bold and powerful shade. Leonardo da Vinci was the first artist to declare that black was not a true color, and Isaac Newton agreed that it was no color at all. Mothers shudder when their daughters start wearing black in their teenage years, although it's now so accepted as a fashion shade that even toddlers are being dressed in it; while filmmakers, television executives, and painters have all come to prefer the bright vibrancy and look-at-me qualities of the color wheel over the years.

Aesthetes have a saying: there is no gray area with black. It is a shade you either love with a passion or quietly dislike. Those who love it happily allow it to dominate their lives, reveling in its drama, sophistication, and monastic simplicity. Those who dislike it avoid it much of the time, carefully stepping around its heaviness in favor of cheerier, more colorful hues.

To understand the divisive effect of black you need to go back through history, to times when black was less of a status symbol and more of symbolic one. During the early Christian period, black was associated with darkness, death, evil, danger and was linked to hell and the devil. At various times black has also been associated with witchcraft. In the Middle Ages it began to gain popularity when black knights started wearing it to disguise their identity. In the 16th and 17th centuries, black became the ultimate color to live your life by; beloved by people like John Calvin who was so fond of its simplicity he established a black-and-white theocracy in 16th-century Geneva in which followers (in a Henry Ford-style philosophy) could wear any color as long as it was black. A century later, in England, Oliver Cromwell also announced that it was the only righteous color. In fact, such was black's popularity during the puritanical 17th century that author Michael Pasture in his book Black: The History of Colour wrote that people developed something of a "chromo-phobia" in their aversion to color. It was, he says, "a great century for black."

It was around this same time that printing began to influence the world, ushering in a new era of communication. Black ink on white paper changed the way we articulated ideas and disseminated information, and it was because of the spread of printing that black achieved dominance in both books and art prints.

Today, black has become emblematic of modernity. Dignified, dramatic, and full of depth, glamour, and character, it is, and will always be, "the new black."

Symbolic connotations attached to black

Formality, sophistication, elegance, wealth, power, modernity, sex, style, mourning, mystery, rebellion, conventionality

Black paint by any other name

Hudson, Hound, Thoroughbred, Urban Living, Architect's Glasses, Floor Plan, Tea Kettle, Truffles, Chateau, Chanel, Carbon Copy, Memorable, Magistrate, Dressage Boots, Double Bass, Writing On The Wall, Typewriter Keys, Chocolate Torte, Chalkboard, Atlantic, Aniseed, Licorice, Picture Frame, Timber Shutters, Tuxedo, Black Jack, Ballgown, Caviar, Oxford Scholar, Gravel, Anchor, Space, Black Berry, Three-Piece Pin Stripe, Satin, Sign, Wrought Iron, New York Wardrobe, Black Is Back

"I've been forty years discovering that the queen of all colors is black."

Renoir

CLASSIC

JASPER CONRAN
LONDON, UK

Refined and quietly dignified while still having a certain dramatic presence, the provenance of the classic black-and-white look lies partly in the quiet grace and understated elegance of Georgian architecture, with its classical proportions, and partly in the fine tailoring and masculine palettes of British tailoring, with its handsome lines. Think of the pleasing symmetry and forms of Bath's or Ireland's gracious Georgian architecture and then think of the sublime detailing and precise cut of a Savile Row suit and you'll have the foundations of the classic black-and-white look. It's architecturally strong but devoid of embellishment, and seemingly simple but based on carefully thought-out forms. In essence, it's simplicity of the most sophisticated kind. Polished to perfection, it's about structure and style rather than artifice and extravagance.

One of the masters of this classic look is leading British designer Jasper Conran, son of the legendary designer Sir Terence Conran, who has established a reputation for sophisticated simplicity and sublime lines in not only suiting but also fragrances, furniture, interiors, and homewares, including collections for Wedgwood china, Waterford Crystal, and Designers Guild. Conran's signature aesthetic mixes classic British elegance with a cheeky irreverent attitude and is shown to best effect at his flagship store in Sackville Street, in London's Mayfair.

Located—fittingly—in the heart of the most prestigious British gentleman's tailoring district, where it has become an iconic part of the sartorial landscape, this store clearly reflects the strong British tailoring for which Conran is so renowned. But what is interesting is that this flair for

Black and white is one of the most sophisticated and timeless design combinations there is. Think of an elegant hallway dressed in black and white or a striking staircase with sculptured white steps and an intricate black balustrade, or a cool white drawing room with a dramatic black fireplace—and black wing armchairs either side, as seen here in Jasper Conran's store.

Photography courtesy of Jasper Conran

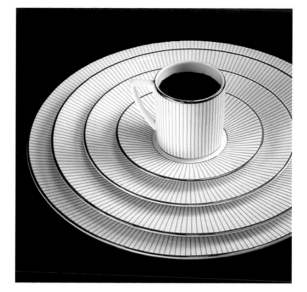

tailoring is present in not only the men's and women's suiting but also in the pared-back interior design, with its elegant lines and monochromatic palette. It's a modern interpretation of the tailoring ethic that has always imbued his work, but it's still finished with the same refined style. Both garments and store (including the homewares collections) are designed in restrained charcoal grays, British navies, off-whites, and ivories, while patterns, if present, are in pinstripes, soft bird's-eye spots, and windowpane checks.

It's a subdued look that is still eye-catching in theatrical style and it reflects Conran's understanding of not only textiles and British tradition but also the elegance and order that comes with the pairing of the two opposites—dramatic suit black and crisp, business-shirt white. Truly classic. Truly monochromatic magic.

The intricate silver-gray lacework of the striking staircase in the black-and-white hall of Jasper Conran's Sackville Street store echoes the black balustrades often seen on London's elegant, inner-city terraces.

London is famous for its love of black and white. The two contrasts are often used in the city's architecture, interior design, and streetscaping—think of the black iron gates, the balconies and balustrades, the sinuous black streetlamps, the graphic black signs, the black-and-white checkerboard paths, halls and entrances, and the dignified front doors. Black and white are also readily found in the fabrics and fashion, the cars—think of London's black cabs—and even in the famous pageantry, although of course in the latter situation they're also joined by a saturation of red.

FIFTH AVENUE APARTMENT
NEW YORK CITY, USA

New Yorkers are very fond of black and white. It's an urban thing. They particularly like black because it never shows the dirt and always looks stylish (and expensive). But they're also partial to white, especially in interiors, where they tend to pair it with grays, chocolates, and other neutral shades.

If you want to know where they get their inspiration, you need only look at the New York skyline, which is a Gothamesque movie set of monochromatic lines and forms that merge together to create a cinematic ode to sharp urban style.

This Fifth Avenue penthouse is pure Manhattan. Dressed in graphic blacks and whites, it's a reflection of its glamorous surroundings. It's also the perfect abode for its two owners, who are imbued with exceptionally good taste—not only in interiors, but also furniture and fashion. When it came time to renovate this residence, located high above Fifth Avenue with compelling views of the city skyline and Central Park below, they chose the high-profile Dutch designer Piet Boon, who is also renowned for his exceptionally good taste. Boon's signature style could be described as luxurious simplicity—he is famous for interiors that are understated but high on style—and he took to the Fifth Avenue project with relish.

The brief from the owners was to create a "Zen-like sanctuary;" an almost meditative space where the family could retreat at the end of each day and not only come together in a comfortable and welcoming environment but also regain some energy after working in the frazzled pace of Manhattan. Boon answered the brief by designing spaces that made the most of the natural light and extraordinary views of Central Park but were also calming places to relax in. He used acres of white to achieve both and also injected the spaces with splashes of urban black. It was the interior opposite of the iconic New York scene in *Breakfast at Tiffany's*, where Audrey Hepburn wears a little black dress with a string of pearls: here the "dress" is white and the accessories are all black.

Photography courtesy of Matthijs van Roon and Mandy Pieper

Everything from the walls to the ornate ceilings, the windows and window coverings, the bedrooms, the kitchen, the chaise longues, and most of the carpets are outfitted in serene, stylish white. The "accessories"—the grand doors to the graphic fireplaces, the elegant circular ottomans, the occasional chairs, and even the floorboards in the dining room, where the drama is heightened by more black—were styled in New York's favourite shade.

Photography by Janelle McCulloch

FASHION EDITOR'S APARTMENT
NEW YORK CITY, USA

It is no coincidence that those who work in fashion are drawn to black and white. The legendary French designer Coco Chanel was a firm advocate of the two tones, pinning white camellias on black lapels, blackening the toes of her beige shoes, constructing soft tweed suits in black-and-white checks, creating two-tone handbags, and of course creating the ultimate ode to black—the little black dress, which she felt was best worn with a long string of white pearls.

Chanel's friendly rivals Christian Dior and Yves Saint Laurent were also firm exponents of the monochromatic look, while Karl Lagerfeld and his contemporaries are now continuing the black-and-white tradition in their modern-day collections. Designers love the stylish dichotomy of black and white because it grabs attention from the moment it walks out onto the catwalk (or the street), and is always timeless, and certainly always chic. It stands out—effortlessly.

This New York abode is a perfect example of the passion that fashionistas have for the enduring style of black and white. Located close to the famous Flatiron Building and owned by a journalist who works as a fashion editor for a well-known magazine, it reflects the monochromatic qualities that sartorial types love in their interiors as much as their wardrobes.

With a bedroom dressed in Ralph Lauren's latest "Black Sands" collection, a living room chandelier beribboned with a black velvet tie, pinboards embellished with clippings on black and white in fashion and film, and chairs swathed in stripes, zebra prints, or Hollywood-style buttons, it's an ode to the glamour and elegance of monochromatic style.

Like many New York apartments, the space is small—indeed, it is barely bigger than a studio—and there is only room for so many pieces, so everything in it has been chosen with care. Many of the pieces serve double functions: the ivory-and-black suitcases serve as a stylish coffee table and look fabulous with a silver tray full of martini glasses on them, lamps serve as statement pieces, and even handbags, most in black and white, are left in strategic position to "accessorize" the space.

But what really refines the apartment and brings it all together in a crisp, chic package is the fact that everything is in black and white. The monochromatic tones both simplify and highlight the space, which is somewhat akin to a gallery. Although there isn't much in this tiny Manhattan home, what is there makes it beautiful.

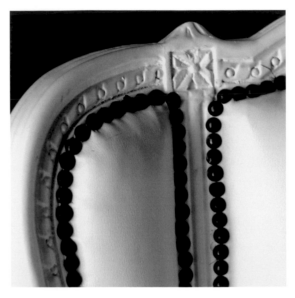

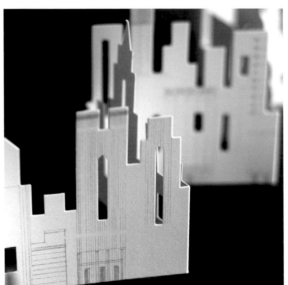

Audrey Hepburn, summer 1957

It's all here in BLACK & WHITE

Fashion's enduring love affair with black and white has produced some iconic moments: think back to Cecil Beaton's costumes for *My Fair Lady* in 1964; Truman Capote's Black and White Ball two years later; or the ea...

by the timeless image Irving Penn, the e London, and even th

baroque Velours toujours spendues

Be yourself. There is something that you can do better than any other. Listen to the inward voice and bravely obey that.

[Unknown]

ACE HOTEL NEW YORK 29TH AT B'WAY

Des jan Nuée de mouss Mancl Cols de re

PETER BEATON NANTUCKET

Janelle McCulloch
EDITOR / PHOTOGRAPHER
Apartment 10, 47 Rockley Road
South Yarra, Victoria, 3141
Australia
janelle.mcculloch@bigpond.com

MANHATTAN PIED-À-TERRE
NEW YORK CITY, USA

New Yorkers are not backward when it comes to being forward, especially when it relates to architecture and interior design. Some of America's most innovative projects are being developed in the city that never sleeps, and this striking pied-à-terre by visionary designer Charles Allem (of leading firm CAD International), which he designed for himself to retreat to whenever he was in town on business, is testament to New York City's extraordinary creativity.

Swathed in layers of black-and-white stripes, the interior is so graphic it could be inspired by the city's famous cartoons or old film noir classics. In fact, the residence was designed to echoes the lines of the highly defined city outside—framed beautifully in the apartment's windows—where horizontals and verticals rule the Manhattan skyline. Allem is a firm fan of monochromatic graphics, especially when used in a minimalist fashion. "It creates harmony," he says, "and keeps everything connected, while making a room dynamic and explosive."

The 1700-square-foot residence on upper Fifth Avenue started out as a two-bedroom apartment. Most people would have been happy with the floor plan, retaining the extra guest bedroom for, well, guests and family. Not Allem. He argues there are beautiful hotels in his part of New York, in which guests will no doubt feel far more comfortable, and so he did something that would shock most New Yorkers: he removed the second bedroom. The result is a luxurious space—and a spacious master suite—that suits this sybaritic designer down to the ground. In fact, he's so enamored with luxury in the home, he even designed his bedroom to resemble a five-star hotel suite, complete with a sitting corner with desk and an inviting TV lounge area.

What really sets this residence apart, however, is the stripes—big, bold, hand-painted horizontal stripes—running right through the apartment, including the office area. For some, these might seem too bold, too, well, stripy, but Allem has cleverly toned them down with the use of equally dramatic vintage furniture, including four glamorous white-leather ottomans (used as dining chairs), graphic black-and-white slipper chairs, a black writing desk, and a kidney-shaped sofa—which are all, interestingly, from the 1950s and 60s. The two—apartment and its pieces—offset each other and seem to "calm" each other down by virtue of being the same dramatic shades. It's an interesting approach to interior design and it certainly works. The place is magnificent.

Allem believes it works because the dominant theme is black and white. The black, he says, which even extends to the floor, unifies the space, while the white brings light and presence to the interior. But he also argues that the space is well edited. There is little clutter, and each piece of furniture serves more than one purpose. As a space—and certainly as a pied-à-terre—it's marvelously multifunctional: a harmonious ode to living well in the city that knows how to do just that.

Photography by Tim Lee

Photography by Tim Lee and Janelle McCulloch

Photography by Janelle McCulloch

SPACE/POLIFORM

The Italians are renowned for their style, not only in fashion but also in furniture; although you could add cars and films to this list as well. Companies such as B&B Italia, Zanotta, Kartell, and Poliform have been redefining style in interiors for some time now; their sleek modern shapes walking a fine—and beautiful—line between sexy and sophisticated. From sofas that puff their chests out to show their full personality to ottomans and chaises that almost purr to express their relaxation factor, Italian furniture is fast showing the rest of the design world how things are done.

One company that has realized the strength in Italian—and indeed European—style and decided to create a business out of it is Space Furniture, an Australian company that now specializes in the world's most beautiful and extraordinary furniture collections. Stocking some of Europe's most legendary design names, Space has achieved such a reputation for fine lines and elegant pleasures (although some clients call them "decadent pleasures") that it has now become as famous as the brands it showcases.

So just why are these brands so extraordinary? What makes them dominate magazine editorials and pique the interest of designers, journalists, and architects alike? Well, let's take B&B Italia. This Italian company has four main collections: the classic B&B Italia Collection; the Maxalto Collection, which revisits classic themes with contemporary flair; the Project Collection, which consists of contemporary minimalist furniture for commercial uses; and the newly expanded Outdoor Collection.

Of these four, you need only look at any one to see what the fuss is about. In the Maxalto Collection, for example, sinuous and linear sofas stand as statement pieces, like a design exclamation mark in the middle of a space. The Amoenus range in particular includes a streamlined sofa and a circular ottoman-sofa, both in a strong monochrome palette, that have so much personality they could almost be considered another guest in the room.

The Maxalto Alcova bed, meanwhile, is billed as a modern interpretation of a classic canopy bed, but has nothing of the old-fashioned tweeness of a traditional four-poster. For a start, it's made to be the star of the bedroom and is made to stand alone in the centre of the room, if you so desire. And its materials, which include leather, brushed oak, or fabric, are not the kind to shrink like a decorating wallflower into a corner.

Then there are pieces, such as the B&B Italia Lazy Chair and Table, which aren't lazy at all but rather straight-backed and smart; the Maxalto Clio chair; the Maxalto Max table and Peplo chair; and the Poliform Ubik wardrobe, which is the kind of wardrobe you'd tend to find in a movie star's Hollywood Hills home.

A Maxalto chair: simple but oh-so-sexy. And surprisingly comfortable—its black (or white) curves mold to the human to offer a sleek fit.

But while these pieces and collections all deserve a place in design history, what really makes them intriguing is that most of them are either designed in black or white—or designed to sit perfectly in black or white spaces. Some of them are colored, of course, but by and large the most striking designs are in rich black or cool white.

Why are the Europeans so enamored with black and white? Well, many believe it's because black and white never go out of style, and so in designing collections in monochrome tones, designers are ensuring their work will still be fashionable in one, two, or even ten years' time. The furniture styles might be ultra-modern, but the monochromatic finishes make them instant classics.

The B&B Italia Lazy chairs and Lens table: a vision of modernity in ice white.

Photography courtesy of Space Furniture, Australia.

The designers of these extraordinary pieces often take their inspiration from the urban lines of the world's most beautiful cities. Here, it's easy to see why the Maxalto Max table and Peplo chairs fit so well into a period Parisian apartment, even though they are far more modern than the century-old space—their lines and coloring are so very Parisian in style.

Photography courtesy of Space Furniture and Janelle McCulloch

Photography courtesy of Poliform, Australia.

The Maxalto Alcova bed, a statement piece that can easily stand on its own in a room—and does.

Photography courtesy of Space Furniture, Australia.

LE DOKHAN'S
PARIS, FRANCE

Trocadéro Dokhan's, or Le Dokhan's as it is known, is an enchanting slice of Paris captured in the form of a hotel. Tucked away in a quiet street near the Eiffel Tower in the 16th arrondissement, it is Paris as you've always imagined it to be—at least when it comes to hotels.

Designed by Frédéric Méchiche and beloved by the international fashion set (Armani books out the entire hotel for all his staff each Fashion Week), it is a flirtatious fantasy of line, form, tone, and style, each element carefully coordinated to create the ultimate in Parisian chic.

The overriding look at Le Dokhan's is, of course, black and white, although the way the monochrome tones are presented varies from room to room. There are black-and-white checks in the entrance, bold black-and-white stripes on the exterior awnings, and finer black-and-white stripes in the foyer hall. The chairs in the main sitting room, meanwhile, are in gray-and-white stripes, which better suit the pale mauve-and-cream walls.

One journalist called it "early neo-classical bonbonniére" and it certainly feels like a Parisian-style sweet box: glamorous and sugary and utterly irresistible.

In a subtle but extremely clever way the interior at Le Dokhan's echoes the highly stylized and oh-so-elegant streetscapes of Paris. The black doors, the stripes, the carefully designed lines of sight, and even the color palette—black and white with more black and white, alongside a little green, gold, and mauve—reflect the aesthetic of the city outside.

The black-and-white-striped columns of the famous forecourt, or cour d'honneur, at the far end of the Palais Royal is one of the most photographed places in Paris, next to the Eiffel Tower and the riverside paths that meander along the Seine. Still striking years after it was created, even with the weathering of the materials, it is loved by children and adults alike. It has also inspired a long list of other iconic places to follow suit, from hotels such as the Le Dokhan's to cafés, bars, and even fashion collections.

Photography by Janelle McCulloch

WRITER'S HIDEAWAY
MELBOURNE, AUSTRALIA

Tucked away in a tree-lined avenue of inner-city Melbourne, a city with distinct European sensibilities, is an apartment that reflects the equally distinct European sensibilities of its owner, a writer who has lived in Paris, London, and Scandinavia.

The author of a number of books on architecture and design, her fascination for fine lines—of both the building and literary kind—is clearly apparent in the interior design, which is peppered with both books and architectural vignettes, from paper skylines of New York to plaster-of-Paris Parisian façades.

Having long been an advocate of the black-and-white look (her previous jobs included stints as a fashion writer and magazine editor), she naturally gravitated toward this monochrome aesthetic when it came to decorating her apartment. Working in magazines means being saturated with colors, fonts, and images all day long, and she began to long for the clarity, simplicity, cleanliness, and easy-on-the-eye palette of pure black and white in her home life; the latter providing much-needed visual and aesthetic relief from the former.

When she bought the apartment it consisted of the bare bones: a plain living room, a plainer bedroom, a dull bathroom, and a large kitchen, which, strangely, was the only room that had been renovated by the previous owners and was surprisingly chic with its French-bistro-style design. Taking a cue from this kitchen she redesigned the rest of the apartment in the same style.

She transformed the living room into a French-style salon, which artfully combined the functions of a sitting room, writing room, library and living area, and detailed the space with books and treasures from her travels around the world. She also selected furniture that was "light", both on the eye and on the arm, such as wicker chairs, low-slung ottomans, and a chaise longue, all of which could be moved easily to reconfigure the room when entertaining guests.

The result is a space that's multi-functional but also imbued with the owner's personality. It's also full of inspiration—from books to photographs to mood boards full of favorite clippings—making it the perfect haven for a writer in constant search of ideas, whether in black and white or living color.

Melburnians are famous for their love of black, which is evident in both their wardrobes and their design. The city is an urban ode to the drama of dark hues, and white is eventually allowed into the mix, which makes for an elegantly graphic statement of sophistication. Talk about a chic city.

Photography by Janelle McCulloch

SCHOOL
HE GROVE
ECHURCH
CHOOL
NKWICK
CHOOL
HNICAL
LLEGE
ANNIE LEIBOVITZ WOMEN SUSAN SONTAG
ARCHITECTURAL
GRAPHIC STANDARDS

DESIGNER'S SANCTUARY
MIAMI, USA

Briggs Edward Solomon is a man who loves monochrome tones. Black and white shades make up much of the design repertoire in his interior design practice, Briggs Edward Design. Black and white, he says, are enduring and timeless, and using them together in rooms not only creates a sense of order and calm, but imbues spaces with instant sophistication.

Take his own residence, for example. The distinguished, black-and-white-styled home in the Coral Gables area of Miami is a pocket of pure serenity in a bustling tropical metropolis. Typographical posters hang beside whimsical black-and-white prints, striped rugs create interest on floors, and quirky black accessories (think top hats and African masks) give the interior design an added graphic punch.

The space works because the base note is white, which creates a seamless flow of pale elegance throughout the home, like a blank canvas upon which to begin painting. These pale spaces are then grounded by the flecks of black, which break up the patterns and lend weight to the "whiteness." The pockets of black also give the eye respite from all the white by offering objects to focus upon. Together, contrast between black and white create decorating magic. Talk about having an impact.

Modern spaces can sometimes be beautiful but austere. Briggs Edward Solomon has overcome this by using texture and contrasts to create a place that's modern yet still warm and inviting. Traditional pieces mix easily with contemporary materials, and flea market finds look elegant beside funky and whimsical furniture. Hard materials play against soft, just as white plays against black.

Photography by Briggs Edward Solomon

FASHIONABLE RETREAT
MIAMI, USA

People who love fashion and glamour tend to be drawn to black and white. They are the traditional shades of fashion and glamour, after all. Just think of Hollywood and the Oscars, or black-tie nights and Paris catwalk shows. Most designers and aesthetes are well aware of how black and white offer a short-cut to style. They murmur "elegance" and "sophistication" without having to say very much at all.

This Miami residence attests to that fact. Designed with classic black-and-white tailoring for a couple enamored with fashion, it is dignified, stylish, quietly glamorous, and beautifully tasteful, not to mention very chic. Conceptualized by Florida designer Briggs Edward Solomon, it was conceived to be a home where the owners could retreat to from the heat and pace of Miami.

The two main shades are, of course, black and white, which offer welcome respite from the bright colors outside, but there are also a few neutrals to bring the glamour back down to earth. Briggs Edwards Solomon loves to inject high-gloss spaces with low-key rusticity. He believes that by injecting a subtle earthiness—or as he calls it, "an earthy elegance"—into the swathes of monochrome, it keeps the spaces relaxed and easy to be in. Thus, a white dining room is grounded by an enormous old timber table, and a writing corner is given gravitas by a charming printer-style desk and schoolhouse chair. Antiques and modern pieces sit side by side in perfect harmony: the old with the new, glamour alongside flea-market frippery.

Photography by Briggs Edward Solomon

Briggs Edward Solomon is known for his penchant for the unexpected and will often go to extraordinary lengths to source pieces from far-flung markets and unusual stores. But with this design project he has excelled himself and the residence is brimming with extraordinary pieces. From wooden folk art to French walnut tables, antique hat stands to vintage wall clocks, the house feels like a gallery to style and good taste. No wonder the owners love coming home at the end of the day.

Miami *is perhaps better known for its ice-cream shades and tropical palettes, but look closely and you'll see quite a lot of black and white in the urban landscape.*

Photography by Janelle McCulloch

COUNTRY

THE WHITE HOUSE
DAYLESFORD, AUSTRALIA

On the surface, black and white don't seem to suit country life as much as they do urban environments, perhaps because they blend into urban environments so much better. However if you look closely in the country you'll actually spot a great deal of the monochrome tones.

Black gumboots or riding boots can often be found lined up beside black front or double stable doors. Grand black or white Aga stoves can often be seen in grand (and small) country kitchens, ready to cook delicious, old-fashioned country feasts. Black-and-white-checked floors can be spotted in country house halls, leading to distinguished black-bookshelf-lined libraries where gracious, white sofas or black wing chairs sit aside cozy black fireplaces. And black thoroughbreds can often be seen kicking up their heels while black-and-white collie dogs wag their tails ready for farm work and black cats sit quietly on hay bales, silently surveying the whole scene.

Black and white do indeed have their special place in the country, and when done well, can look just as effective as strong, bright colors—perhaps even more so because they don't fight with the scenery for attention but rather allow the beauty of the countryside to show through.

This charming 1850s miner's cottage, located in the former gold mining region of Victoria, Australia, is indicative of the way black and white can be used to great effect in a rural setting. Bought by a Melbourne interior designer with an eye for stylish pieces—her store, Empire Vintage 111, is an Australian Mecca for magazine stylists and aesthetes—the cottage was fairly "vintage" itself when she first laid eyes on it, although it had undergone several metamorphoses under its previous owner, who had successfully lifted it from shack to chic. But when the current owner came in, she saw the potential for even more beauty and rolled up her stylish sleeves to get stuck in.

Photography by Janelle McCulloch

Using her talents for sourcing unusual vintage furniture and pieces from markets, collections, and country stores all around Victoria, she slowly began to amass a booty that would have impressed an auctioneer at Sotheby's, all set aside ready to be shipped up to the cottage when the time was right.

In the meantime, both she and her builder began work on further restoring the miner's cottage. Stripping it back to its bare bones, they reconfigured some of the rooms so that one of the bedrooms became a luxurious black-and-white bathroom, complete with fireplace and claw-footed bath in its center, and another became a handsome black library, also with a fireplace and—the showpiece—a stunning wallpaper made to look like black-and-white books; although there's also a real bookshelf to keep the bibliophiles happy. The rear of the house, meanwhile, was

transformed into a single grand room with an open Parisian bistro-style kitchen, a chic little sitting room, an irresistible living room complete with comfy club chairs and sofas with cheeky Union Jack throws, and a sun-filled dining space.

Black and white were chosen as the dominant tones in order to keep everything very clean and streamlined. These shades also served to visually organize the vignettes that pepper every corner, from vintage papers to artworks, maps, prints, books, and even old typewriters and ex-industrial factory furniture pieces.

Although called The White House, it's not entirely white. There's also quite a lot of black—and red and blue. The base palette is black and white, with red introduced as an accent color to lift the rooms from what could otherwise be a glamorous but slightly cool photographic look and make them pop with unexpected color.

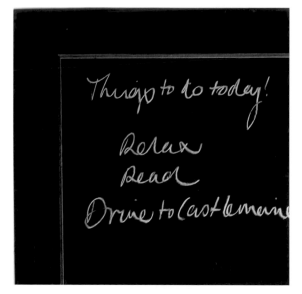

The beauty of using black and white in country interiors is that the contrast of these two strong opposites prevents country interiors from sinking too much into a clichéd twee look. If you want to imbue your country house with a monochromatic elegance, just start with the basics—black and white. If you're a traditionalist, opt for lots of patterns in different styles—broad checks, ginghams, and toiles look gorgeous. If you're more modern, go bold with blocks of black and white (gloss if possible), and if you want to do something truly extravagant, introduce a zebra or cow print.

The owner's love of words and wit and combining them together in cheeky interiors is shown here, in the garden bedroom, where black-and white pages from a horticultural book have been tacked in a charming fashion to create a literary "picture" on the wall.

Some of the inspiration for The White House may well have come from its village surrounds. Located in Daylesford, a charming settlement tucked away in the former goldfields of Victoria, the house seems to take many of its decorating cues from the town's plentiful vintage elements—and the lovely gray, white, black, and gilt color schemes of the stores in the main street. For rental enquiries, please refer to www.empirevintage.com.au/ thewhitehousedaylesford.

DESIGNER'S FARMHOUSE
WOODEND, AUSTRALIA

It may be due to the predominance of green, which saturates country scenes, from forests to farmland and everything in between, and the myriad other colors, including reds, pinks, and lilacs, that saturate country gardens, but black and white sometimes take a back seat in the design of many country homes. And that's a shame, because when used well they can transform spaces into soft, subdued places perfect for country living and act as an ideal canvas for Mother Nature's rich shades that come through the windows.

This century-old farmhouse, which is known as Fern Vale Farm and located down the end of a holly lane like some fabulous, fairytale-style hideaway, shows how black and white can be applied to verdant country settings to enchanting effect. Owned by Melbourne-based interior designer, Jane Charlwood, the house was a dark, cluttered bed-and-breakfast when she purchased it, with none of the light and style it has now. Redesigning an old country house involves different challenges from a modern city abode, but Charlwood fixed the issues of poky bedrooms and labyrinthine halls by reconfiguring the floor plan to make the principal rooms bigger, which she then opened up further with hundreds of liters of white paint. Window frames, walls, even the floorboards in some rooms, were all finished in a chalky, eggshell white, which had the effect of transforming the house into a gallery fit for the furniture that was to follow. The whitewash also allowed the lush green, hedge-edged garden to be seen through white windows, which framed the setting beautifully.

Photography by Janelle McCulloch

The most important thing about using black and white in the country is that there should be a spirit of traditionalism, even in the more modern rural retreats. Beds can be contemporary (although they look better when they're iron or four-poster), but it's far more true to the country to dress them in white linen and then cover them in charcoal-black or pale gray blankets.

When it comes to window seats and cushions, some of the prettiest coverings are black-and-white French ticking fabrics, as shown here, in Jane Charlwood's farmhouse. And statement pieces such as wing armchairs, chaise longues, and ottomans can be upholstered in gingham-inspired black-and-white checks for true country drama—the bigger the check, the greater the drama.

Fireplaces, meanwhile, stand as simple but striking silhouettes when black hearths are etched in white surrounds and then topped with black mantles, while country kitchens look magnificent with long black timber tables, big white enamel sinks, and oversized black or white Aga stoves topped with black pots, simmering away. Lastly, in the bathrooms, classic claw-footed baths can look beautiful when painted black on the outside and then positioned beside ornate black mirrors, elegant black folding screens, or even fireplaces to create a sanctuary of style.

COUNTRY LODGE
MALLACOOTA, AUSTRALIA

Karbeethong Lodge sits on one of the prettiest inlets in Australia—a picturesque swish of water that's so quiet, that when the pelicans land everyone looks up to see what made the noise. Not surprisingly the nearby town of Mallacoota has been a haven for artists, writers, musicians, and creative souls for many a decade. This lodge has been a refuge for those seeking a quiet place for contemplation or inspiration away from the bustle and constant cacophony of the city. And when you look inside, you can see why. It's a lodge made for lounging.

Decked out in blacks, whites, and reds, the lodge is gracious but easy-going, dramatic yet also down-to-earth. Parts of it are formal without being stuffy (there is a piano in the corner), while others are breezy and casual without being bland. The dining room is a divine space full of gorgeous lines, while the living room is a Mecca for checks. The bedrooms are miniature pleasure zones in themselves, with layers of fine gingham adding to the country spirit.

The lodge, and its interior design, is a tribute to Sydney businesswoman Rosemary Luker, who bought it with her husband Russell so they could have a place to get away—and offer to others to stay for a small price. When she first assessed the interior, however, the design was all a bit "cabbage rosey," says Luker, and a lot of the clutter needed to go. So out went the "stuff" and in came the statement pieces. The rich black-and-white paneled timber walls were left intact and a beautiful tomato-red paint was applied to the top half to create visual interest and impact. The paint was mixed especially for the residence by Aalto, a specialist paint store loved by designers. "I wanted it to be very red, like crushed tomatoes," says Luker. "It needed to be quite saturated because the wood was so dark in parts and so pale in others."

The effect worked. The walls came alive. Windows were also outlined in high-gloss white to add to the zing. And then when the new furniture was moved in—boldly upholstered armchairs and sofas in broad, cheeky checks—the lodge took on a new life.

Photography by Antoine Rozes and Jenny Wiedermann

TOWN AND COUNTRY STYLE
COLLECTIONS

Town and Country Style is a relatively new Australian store that has rapidly achieved an enviable reputation in the media for extraordinary design and extraordinary styling. With a penchant for black and white—and variations of these tones, such as French gray, beige, taupe, and cream—the store's owner has become as famous for her delicious merchandising and witty displays as she has for her taste in furniture and homewares.

Heavily influenced by the French look, Town and Country Style takes bits from the Paris school of decorating—such as the chalked-out maps of the Right Bank on the dark-gray timber-paneled walls and the chalked outline of a French café on the far kitchen wall—and mixes them flirtatiously with influences from Cape Cod, New York, New England—grand, black Manhattan bookshelves and cabinets—and even quirky looks from London—the wallpapered walls, which are covered in pages ripped from classic literature texts.

Town and Country Style's staff are also not afraid to frame pages of print to create a side table of classic lines (further enhanced by a French quote chalked across the wall above them) or take the covers of books and turn them around so that their black spines become a beautiful publishing-inspired gallery.

It's a wonderfully outlandish look that, admittedly, is jazzed up a little for retail sales, but there's no reason others can't emulate it for their own homes. And many have already done so. Using pieces from Town and Country Style's collections, they have created whimsical little "Town and Countries" in their own abodes—full of wit, humor, and style. And all in monochrome.

Photography by Janelle McCulloch

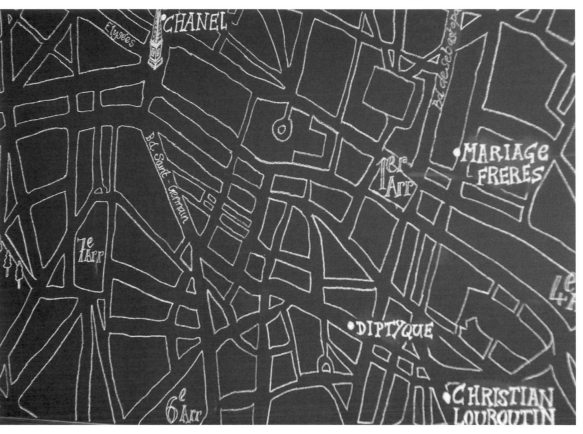

COAST

ISLAND HIDEAWAY
FLORIDA KEYS, USA

You wouldn't think there was any place for black and white down on the Florida Keys. It seems to be more of a Caribbean environment where joyous, bubblegum colors saturate the landscape. However, there's one corner of the Keys where subdued shades reign. It's a corner where everything is low-key and sophisticated, a place where the only outlandish colors likely to be found are in the captivating sunsets that sink over the islands each night.

It's a pocket of perfection known as Islamorada, or Village of Islands, and it's a place within this perfect pocket called Maroni House that is arguably one of the most beautiful places on the Keys.

Set a few sandy steps back from the beach under a copse of shady palm trees, Maroni House is what perfect beach houses are supposed to look like: compact on the outside, spacious on the inside, embellished with a wonderful wraparound veranda for staring out to sea, enhanced with French doors that lead out to the aforementioned veranda, and imbued with a colonial-style charm that makes you feel you're somewhere truly exquisite. The real beauty of Maroni House, though, is its understated nature. And this is where the monochromatic palette comes in.

Photography by Janelle McCulloch

Maroni's owners, who also own several other beach houses in this luxury retreat known as The Moorings, deliberately built the house in the classic beach house style, with a white-timber exterior, a low-slung roofline, and a wraparound white-timber veranda to sit on and gaze out to sea through the frame of palm trees. It's no coincidence that the timber chairs on the decked veranda are covered in a pale-beige canvas that's the exact color of the sandy paths and beach in front. It's a decorating ruse that has the effect of keeping everything very low-key, and it also puts the emphasis back onto the landscape, which, in this stunning place, is where it should be.

Inside, the cool, calm, quietly glamorous monochromatic style continues. Dark, high-gloss floorboards run the length of the house, giving the spaces a rich sheen—and allowing for the sand that will inevitably enter—while white, high-gloss French doors allow the rooms to open up unto each other and the deck to create a seamless flow between inside and out. Most of the furniture is dark and colonial in style, which, instead of being too heavy, gives the house a romantic colonial feel.

On the walls, black and white vintage photographs of classic coastal scenes—yachts, beaches, palm trees, and people—lend further glamour, while the furnishings, most of which are in cool neutrals—creams, whites, blacks, and taupes—walk a lovely line between looking impeccably chic and creating a wonderfully casual, laid-back feel.

It's a house where all you want to do is walk in, take off your city clothes, don some flip flops and a favorite old straw hat, and wander down to the white hammock—that's conveniently slung between two palm trees—with a glass of white wine and a classic book and feel blissfully content. For rental enquiries, please refer to www.themooringsvillage.com.

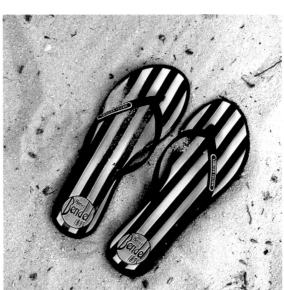

WATERFRONT RETREAT
FLORIDA KEYS, USA

This house may seem like the quintessential tropical hideaway on the outside, framed as it is in a sky soaked with blue, a palm-tree plantation laden with green, and a pink sandy beach held in place with a watermelon and turquoise boat. But venture inside and it becomes a cool oasis of monochrome elegance—and an unexpected respite from the heat of the Florida day.

Photography by Janelle McCulloch

The first inkling that you're about to enter somewhere quite special is the front veranda, which faces the sea (the white and blue reflecting the colors of the water) and is filled with the flotsam and jetsam of coastal life. From the tall jars filled with beautiful white shells to a long timber dining table ready for dinner, the pots full of fragrant bushes—frangipani, orchids, ferns, and hibiscus—that scent the air, mingling with the salt to create a perfume that's distinctly coastal, and the collection of colonial-inspired rattan and timber chairs topped with plump white cushions that offer the perfect dress-circle seats for the show of clouds and light that unfold over the water each day, it's a place where peace of mind and relaxation come easy.

It may have been a deliberate design ruse to tone down the colors for the interior of this sublime white-timber beach house in order to make it more of a serene sanctuary from the tropical paint pots that Mother Nature has splashed around outside, or it may have simply been the owners' preference for understated shades, but the interior of this oceanfront hideaway is very different from the exterior.

Inside, the picture changes slightly, but it's no less easy on the eye. The front living room, a wonderful space enhanced by a fireplace and windows looking out to sea, is testament to both the owners' tastes and their travels around the world. The room is filled with a huge white sofa, an enormous black-and-white replica sailboat, a cozy fireplace, myriad photographs of the family, and intriguing *objets d'art*. Another delightful touch is the dozens of coffee-table books on art, design, architecture, and even surfing placed in neat piles everywhere—many of them with intriguing black-and-white spines—including the famous tome on photographer Helmut Newton that comes with its own impressive stand. The kitchen, too, is an ode to monochrome, with a black dining table and chairs topped with white-tie cushions and a display of white shells and black-and-white family photographs.

It's a house where harmony reigns, thanks to the quietly refined interior design, but it's also a house that's livable, one that's made for family and entertaining and beach life. And those elements are rare to find together. Thanks to the black-and-white palette, the owners have carried off the combination with aplomb.

CARRIAGE HOUSE
NANTUCKET ISLAND, USA

Black and white is rarely associated with the coast—beach interiors tend to veer more toward marine or coastal colors, such as navy, aqua, red, yellow, or all-white. In recent years, however, black and white have found a home in coastal regions as increasing numbers of beach house owners go monochrome in search of a different, and perhaps more sophisticated, look. In fact, black and white work particularly well in coastal environments, and not just because they're distinctly chic; black and white distill forms down to their essence, creating a simplicity that seems to suit coastal spaces.

This house on the island of Nantucket on America's east coast, is a perfect example. Owned by Mrs. Voorhees, a Nantucket local who is involved in both Nantucket realty and the heritage of the island, the residence started life as a carriage house and stables for a grand home nearby. It's a neatly compact building, as carriage houses tend to be, but because of its origins it had a lot of potential for living space, both within the two-story building and outside, in the large courtyard.

Wishing to make the most of its unusual lines and exquisite form, the owner commissioned leading American architect Hugh Newell Jacobsen to redesign the space to make it more open, and also more modern, without losing its character, integrity, or charm.

Jacobsen, who is celebrated for his minimalist style and as well known for his modern pavilion-based residences and simple, gabled, rectangular forms as he is for his love of white, took on the project with a passion. Jacobsen's signature style is deliberately sparse and linear, which serves to highlight the spaces within and without. He endeavors to design buildings that belong in their landscape and enhance the site, rather than overpowering it with bold architecture. Having long been inspired by the outbuildings of rural America—the barns, the detached kitchens, and smokehouses—he, too, saw the potential in the carriage house. Jacobsen didn't shy away from its boxy, awkward form but rather embraced it wholeheartedly.

Working hard to preserve the lines of the house, its linearity, and also its character and origins, Jacobsen let the provenance of the building determine the configuration of the living spaces within. Thus the grand, double carriage doors remained and became a dramatic new entrance to the home—and a secure one as well for when there was no one home. The space behind these enormous white doors became the living room, which was anchored by a geometric black-and-white fireplace and, flanking it either side, two of the most appealing window seats imaginable, both dressed in gracious white cushions and both topping, like the interior design version of a white ice cream on a waffle cone, two beautifully designed wood cupboards. Jacobsen designed the rustic timber cuts to be the only color in this coolly serene room, which is almost a shrine to the beauty of white. Everything from the walls to the floors to the sofas and even the prints, sourced from Le Louvre in Paris, is white. The only things that aren't are the views—which take in the traditional Nantucket shingle house next door—but even that is an elegant gray shade that seems to suit this monastically simple space.

Photography by Janelle McCulloch

The only shot of color in this beautifully monochromatic house is in the library, where the owners' books have been used as a gallery of multi-hued shades. Jacobsen, who is rather fond of libraries (he has a 6,000-volume collection of his own) decided to place such an emphasis on these books that he allowed the bookcases to determine the size and placement of the windows. The result is a space where the books are enhanced and the house falls away elegantly behind them, so that both coexist in perfect alignment. With an almost fanatical attention to the integrity of both the library and the building, Jacobsen has created a space that is at once beautiful and livable.

The islands of Nantucket and neighboring Martha's Vineyard are well known for their monochrome homes. One part that's particularly elegant is the historic Old Town of Edgartown, on the island of Martha's Vineyard, which consists almost solely of white clapboard houses laced with black shutters, thanks to a preservation overlay on the town.

Because of this, the town has a lovely decorum and a rather distinguished air, much like the architectural version of a black-tie dinner where everyone manages to look their best even while dressing like everyone else. There is not a blemish on any gate, façade, or garage. Lamps, front doors, windows, and even picket fences are almost all finished in impeccably kept black and white.

While Edgartown on Martha's Vineyard is famous for its black-and-white architecture, Nantucket is more known for its gray-and-white homes, most of which were built in traditional shingle. There are still a great many places on Nantucket that were designed in black and white, but the classic Nantucket look is beautifully weathered gray shingle, topped with fresh trims of white.

ONE "MO" TIME

MARTHA'S VINEYARD, MA

MERIDIAN

Edgartown, Martha's Vineyard: classic American chic.

THE LANDING
HARBOUR ISLAND, BAHAMAS

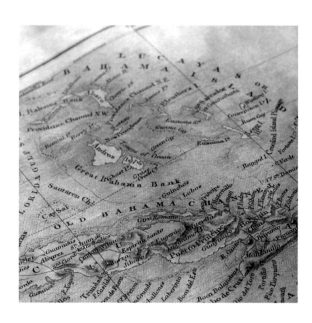

In the late 1990s, Australian businessman Toby Tyler and Bahamian-born New York model Tracy Barry, who had met on a blind date in Sydney, decided to restore an old family estate on Harbour Island, a beautiful out island of the Bahamas. Their original plan had been to sell the estate, which Tracy had inherited, but when they traveled to the island to assess the property and found themselves standing in front of two of the most architecturally significant buildings in the Bahamas, they decided to put down their bags and stay. As Toby says: "I fell in love twice; once with my wife, and then with her island."

With the help of India Hicks, daughter of famed London designer David Hicks (and granddaughter of Lord Mountbatten), they gradually restored the two buildings: an 1820 plantation-style house called The Landing, which is the first sight for visitors as they arrive by water taxi to the island (the only way to reach this idyllic outpost), and the neighboring 1820 property called The Captain's House, which is just as gracious.

Having survived more than a century of weather, the white limestone and clapboard-sided buildings were solid but desperately in need of care after Hurricane Floyd ripped through the island in 1999. Determined to retain the elegant, understated feel of the architecture and its airy breezeways, high ceilings, polished hardwood floors, solid white walls, and wraparound verandas, Toby, Tracy, and India set about restoring the buildings using local craftsmen and the finest materials to create two classic, plantation-style island retreats.

Photography by Janelle McCulloch

Putting the emphasis on blacks, whites, and natural timber tones, in the tradition of colonial homes, the trio left the floorboards in a dark gloss and then painted the rest of the interior, from the floors to the walls and French doors, white. They then set about working on the rooms. For the guest bedrooms, they commissioned dignified, dark four-poster beds and then outfitted each with crisp white linen by Ralph Lauren and layers of cool, cotton netting. Sunlight can be an issue in the Bahamas, so white shutters where engaged to filter the light during the day. At night, black-and-white lamps and white hurricane candles provide a soft, island-style ambiance.

For the reception area, designer India Hicks came up with the idea to draw a whimsical, black-and-white figure on the wall, which gave the hall a sense of humor and wit—and also gave visitors something to smile at when they checked in.

There are many beautiful things about The Landing, but perhaps the most gorgeous are the vignettes that appear when you least expect them. From the handsome black-and-white signs to the quirky labels on Toby's own wine, to the view from the elegantly shuttered balconies and even the staff (including Toby himself who's always ready with a smile), the hotel is a shrine to simplicity and chic island style.

THE RALEIGH
MIAMI, USA

Is there a more glamorous hotel in America than The Raleigh? Perhaps, but there's certainly something very Hollywood about this Miami icon, which is still one of the most impressive sights on South Beach. An architectural symphony of form and line, The Raleigh is famous for many things—the celebrity guests and poolside parties among them—but the one feature it's most famous for is its pool, a sinuous, black-edged baroque form that's as sexy and as curvaceous as the bikini-clad girls down on the beach in front of it. Voted by *Travel & Leisure* magazine as one of the top ten most beautiful pools in the world, it's an Art Deco masterpiece that immediately sets a high-octane level of glamour.

Indeed, so beautiful is The Raleigh's pool that its highly defined, streamlined black lines have been repeated elsewhere in the hotel, most notably around the pool and in the "Oasis," the whimsical adult play area at the rear of the pool deck. Here, scattered between the palm trees like monochromatic confetti, is an irresistible collection of black-and-white striped deckchairs, chaise longues, umbrellas, and private cabanas for guests to play in and upon. Occasionally there's an injection of red, but mostly it's a fantastic picture of perfect black and white forms: graphic, gorgeous, and utterly glamorous.

Photography by Janelle McCulloch

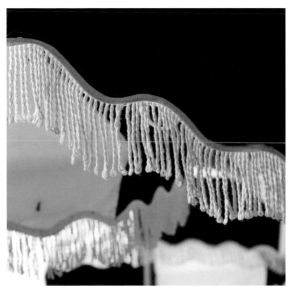

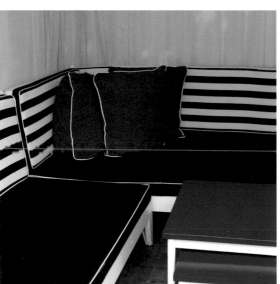

CLIFFTOP HOUSE
PORTSEA, AUSTRALIA

Hidden away on a clifftop path in the tiny but idyllic coastal village of Portsea, in Australia's southern state of Victoria, is a house so quiet you don't even realize it's there. Reached by a sandy track that passes through a series of enchanting white-timber gates, and an equally enchanting series of piers that belong to the houses above them, the residence is a beach shack compared to its neighbors, at least in size, but no less impressive in design. In fact, its proportions are what make it so charming.

The exterior of the house has been constructed from white timber in the traditional beach house style, but what gives it punch is that the poetry of this timber has been punctuated with graceful elongated black shutters that provide a very sophisticated finish. Inside, the black-and-white grace continues, with rooms that are casual and comfortable but carefully coordinated to be chic as well.

Photography by Janelle McCulloch

As you would expect of a beach house, nautical and coastal references pepper the interior design, from miniature wooden sailboats to matching napkins made from black-and-white striped, sailcloth-style canvas. But what really gives this place its whimsy, and its beauty, are the quirky pieces such as the tiny Adirondack chairs, perfect replicas of the classic beach chair, which sit prettily in front of a row of white magazines, or the mini surfboard, complete with red and white stripes, that serves as a bookend to publications on coastal hideaways all over the world. There are even jars of white shells and sand, collected from travels around the world that have been "cataloged" in old apothecary jars, like exotic specimens in a museum, and then labeled according to the beaches they're from, including the Bahamas, Bell's Beach, Whitehaven, Martha's Vineyard, Miami, Hawaii, Tahiti, and Lord Howe Island.

HIGH GLAMOUR

THE INTERNATIONAL
BRIGHTON, AUSTRALIA

Harking back to the days when cocktail cabinets and chaise longues were *de riguer*, High Glamour is all about beautifully refined silhouettes and rich, sophisticated finishes. It's an old-fashioned style of glamour mixed in with modern drama and contemporary sexiness. Think of the soigné settings of the 1920s or the impeccably tailored glamour of 1930s and 40s films crossed with the sleek movie sets and monochromatic wardrobe of films like Brad Pitt and Angelina Jolie's *Mrs and Mrs Smith* or Pierce Brosnan's *The Thomas Crowne Affair* and you have the general idea. It's luxurious, delightful, and "de lovely," as Cole Porter would say.

Many people love High Glamour. They love its cinematic drama, and the sheer wow factor it inevitably creates. But they usually shy away from trying to replicate it in their own homes because they think it's high maintenance—that perhaps they'll need their own Hollywood-style butler to maintain the sheen. In fact, High Glamour is relatively easy to achieve. It's like the architectural version of a tuxedo, or a long, black ball gown. Once you get the formal elements in place, you don't need to do much more other than stand back and stare breathlessly at the effect.

The stunning interior of The International, designed by Melbourne firm Hecker Phelan Guthrie, shows just how glamorous—and easy—the black-and-white Hollywood style can be. A new events center in one of Melbourne's most prestigious suburbs, the venue was designed to have a chic, Chanel-esque feel—although others have commented that it has a more mature, subdued Frank Sinatra kind of flair. As in just add the martini glasses and mix.

The key to its beauty is that everything is heavily edited, and then edited again, so that what remains is the essence of elegance. Once again, it takes its inspiration—or rather, its cue—from the classic movies, where starlets used to stretch languidly on low chaise longues while men in smoking jackets sipped on cocktails behind them. Every piece of furniture was there for a reason—bar carts for cocktails, slipper chairs for chatting or posing, chaises for kissing, mirrors for redoing your lipstick, and small tables for entertaining. Everything was carefully considered and assessed for its image, because in Hollywood even the furniture had to be beautiful.

Photography by Janelle McCulloch

Here, the principles are just the same. The black-and-white, diamond-tiled floor sets the scene from the start, creating a whimsical, harlequin-style base upon which to build the drama. Structured around this are multi-paneled white walls, with Hollywood-style mirrors positioned at strategic intervals; round black ottomans that fit neatly together like a glamorous shamrock; an ornate, black-tiled fireplace; and cream pendant lamps to provide subdued light.

While black and white are the defining characteristics, there is also a significant emphasis on line and form. Streamlined to the point where it has the studied, sophisticated feel of a carefully stage-directed set design, the space is further developed through the use of the gorgeous curves on the mirror, ottomans, lamps, and vases. But while these curves give it form and depth, it's still very much a picture of pure glamour, due to the disciplined use of black and white. There is some color—a Dior-gray sofa here, some verdant palms there—but for the most part it's a gallery to monochromatic glamour.

JK PLACE
FLORENCE, ITALY

The Italians have always known how to put on a show. They don't need to take direction from Hollywood for that. In fact, Hollywood has often gone to Italy to see how La Dolce Vita is done—just think of films like *Roman Holiday* and *The Talented Mr Ripley*.

If there is one place that shows how well the Italians do glamour, it's JK Place in Florence, one of the country's—and perhaps also the continent's—most beautiful hotels. JK Place is testament to the fact that good taste is innate to these stylish people. While many other international hotels go down the chintz or beige-and-chocolate path, JK's designers have opted for a color palette that's a little more original—black and white over a glamorous ice blue.

The monochromatic elegance begins at JK Place with the black-stained timber floors and contrasting white walls, which give the spaces depth and dignity. It's then enhanced by furniture pieces carefully positioned in unexpected configurations—small round black coffee tables are paired with simple cream wing chairs, a black-and-white zebra ottoman rests beside a Dior-gray pinstripe sofa and two elegant white armchairs, and a painting that seems to be nothing but a canvas of matt black hangs beside a gilt-framed line figure in a way that looks utterly magic, with one complementing the other in subtle fashion.

The key to JK Place's sophistication—and design perfection—is the pairing of black and white, which quietly fuses the whole scene in a distinctly elegant way. It's glamour, but it's glamour with a polished, warm persona; it's a space designed to feel very much like someone's home. Of course, it's far more glamorous and dramatic than most people's homes, but the clever combination of intimacy, style, and personal touches—such the throw rugs, the prints, and the accessories—make it terribly inviting anyway.

Hotels can so easily be cold and sterile in their attempts at formality; overly stuffy in some parts of their decor and underdone in others. In contrast, JK Place clearly shows that you can take a public space and make it personal—and truly special.

Photography courtesy of JK Place and Massimo Listri

UMA UBUD
BALI, INDONESIA

Part of the famous, Christine Ong-owned Uma Ubud hotel in Bali's Ubud hinterland, this fabulous bath forms one half of a serene retreat known as a Garden Suite. There are several of these suites at the Uma Ubud, and each of these remarkable spaces focuses on water and the outdoors. On one side is a traditional bedroom, with a canopy bed dressed in peaceful white; on the other an ultra-modern bathroom with a magnificent freestanding bath painted in black. The two seemingly disparate spaces are fused beautifully thanks to a walled, Bali-style outdoor courtyard, that comes complete with fishpond, chairs, and checkerboard terrace.

Of these three spaces, it is perhaps the bathroom that has the most design impact. The astonishingly sleek open-air space looks up to the sky, allowing you to bathe while the cool breezes and sun wash over you from above. The black walls, black tub, and the white drapes that frame the bath combine to create a cool sanctuary—your own personal outdoor spa. What's most beautiful about this tranquil bathing area, though, is the black-and-white checked ottoman, which is upholstered in a fabric directly inspired by a traditional black-and-white fabric used by the Balinese. It's a contemporary space that's influenced by traditional elements: a coolly glamorous retreat that's perfect on a hot Bali day.

Photography by Janelle McCulloch

DESIGNERS GUILD

British design firm Designers Guild is famous for its spectacular patterns and fabrics. One of the foremost international home and lifestyle companies, it's owned by the influential designer Tricia Guild OBE, who is well known for her love of, and use of, colour—the bolder and more flamboyant the better. Think raspberry pinks, tropical tangerines, lustrous turquoises, jewel pinks, and rich Indian reds.

Lesser known is Guild's love of black and white, yet the queen of color adores monochromes and believes they're as important as all the other shades. Black and white is, she says, a classic combination that has been used in art and architecture by everyone from Masaccio to Mondrian to Le Corbusier and beyond.

So when it came time to designing her Amalienborg range, a range inspired by the 18th-century Rococo elegance of royal St. Petersburg and its architecture and decoration, she decided to draw on the pared-back beauty of black and white to create a highly stylized collection. It was a risk, but it paid off, because there is something starkly beautiful about this very special range of fabrics, which do have a certain Russian air in their grandeur and glamour. Featuring ornate patterns, classical Rococo forms, and more stylized graphic images, the Amalienborg collection harks back to a regal time when things were more formal and stately. The effect is dramatic but still dignified, daring yet still executed with class and distinction.

Photography courtesy of Designers Guild

101 HOTEL
REYKJAVIK, ICELAND

You would imagine that the dramatic landscapes of Iceland would inspire some dramatic architecture, and this space proves it. Located in Iceand's capital, Reykjavik, the intriguing 101 Hotel is the creation of owner and designer Ingibjörg S. Pálmadóttir, a graduate from the prestigious Parsons School of Design in New York City.

Pálmadóttir envisaged a place in Reykjavik where people could relax amid luxury that wasn't too intimidating or too over-the-top, a place that reflected the clean lines and monochromatic palette of her country. So she drew up a design for a special hotel, which she called, quite simply, 101. Pálmadóttir chose materials sympathetic to the city surroundings and also to Iceland itself—rustic woods, shiny metals, and textured sands—and then added acres of icy white and volcanic black. The effect was like light on snow: utterly dazzling.

Photography courtesy of 101 Hotel

The hotel was saved from being too glacial and cold with the help of a few carefully thought-out touches, glowing log fireplaces and the rich patina of American oak timber flooring among them. But Pálmadóttir felt it was imperative to retain the graphic black-and-white palette because it was so calming. It also perfectly suited the building the hotel was encased in: a property built in the 1930s in the early Modernist style.

Now, with a hip, black-tiled plunge pool, a cozy lounge with black leather chairs, a sultry billiard room, and a view over the city and Mount Esja under the midnight sun, 101 Hotel has quickly become the coolest place in town.

HABITA MONTERREY
MEXICO CITY, MEXICO

When you think of Mexico you don't necessarily think of sleek lines and pared-back forms, unless of course you're talking about Luis Barragan. One of Mexico's most influential 20th century architects, Barragan is famous for his mastery of space and light and reinvention of the International Style as a spectacular genre of Mexican Modernism. But by and large, Mexico seems to favor other styles of design and architecture, such as the Hacienda, Colonial, and Spanish Colonial styles. However, that was before the Habita Monterrey hotel came along.

One of the most talked-about places in Mexico and, it seems, the world, now that it's been covered extensively by the international design media, the Habita MTY, as it's known, is owned by the Monterrey Grupo Habita, a company that's already designed more than a few of Mexico's most stylish boutique hotels. Designed by Mexican architect Agustín Landa and Parisian interior designer Joseph Dirand, it represents minimalism at its best; indeed, it doesn't even look like a hotel. The lobby is a vision of monochromatic minimalism, where even the reception staff is dressed in white. The keys are curious, oversized metal cylinders with an old-fashioned key attached, and the do-not-disturb signs are heavy metal plaques that are so funky guests have been known to take them home.

The 39 rooms, meanwhile, are crisp pictures of black and white, with low black platform beds, black shutters, and white walls, linen and furniture. Even the accessories are black and white—iPod docking stations, Nokia tablet PCs, and Aesop bath products in the bathrooms.

The international design crowd might dub it "luxuriously austere," but it's neither too luxurious nor too austere. Instead, it treads a lovely line between high-end luxe, design-hotel chic, and low-key comfort. The Habita is entirely habitable. And entirely fabulous.

Photography courtesy of Undine Prohl

LUXURY RESIDENCE
CAPE TOWN, SOUTH AFRICA

This luxurious residence, designed by John Jacob Zwiegelaar of John Jacobs Interiors in Cape Town, is a symphony in elegance. Zwiegelaar's style of work is characterized by his extraordinary range of references, which swing from French neo-classical to contemporary Belgian haute-decoration and even to a Roberto Cavalli-esque rockstar style. His signature look, however, is one defined by monochromatic tones. Zwiegelaar is the master of monochrome and many of his projects are strong on contrasts, leading to a look that's big on glamour and even bigger on eye-popping drama.

In less-skilled hands, the black-and-white look can sometimes appear overworked; for example, if there is too much of one and not enough of the other, the effect can seem unbalanced. Not here. In Zwiegelaar's adept palms, everything has been superbly aligned and beautifully coordinated so that only calm reigns.

The black-and-white walls and floors provide a theatrical backdrop for the cinematic scene that follows, while the black furniture acts as a magnetic focal point and the white accessories provide the visual exclamation mark. Even in the bathroom and kitchen, where corners are crammed with glamorous bits, there is a sense of well-ordered style.

It's a salute to sybaritic style. But more than that it's a salute to the spectacular effect of classic black and white; it's sharp, linear, confident, and heart-stoppingly chic.

Photography courtesy of Sacha Park

ACKNOWLEDGMENTS

The Images Publishing Group and Janelle McCulloch would like to sincerely thank the following designers, hotels, hoteliers and photographers for their kind contribution to this work (in order of appearance):

Maxalto and Space Furniture Australia, the Mondrian Miami, Jasper Conran London, Piet and Karin Boon of Piet Boon Studio BV and photographers Matthijs van Roon and Mandy Pieper, Charles Allem and Mary Matos-Lacasa of CAD International in Miami and photographer Tim Lee, B&B Italia, Kartell, Maxalto and Poliform, Hôtel Sofitel Trocadéro Dokhan in Paris, Briggs E. Solomon of Briggs Edwards Solomon design in Miami, Lyn Gardner of Empire Vintage 111 in Melbourne, Jane Charlwood of Jane Charlwood Design in Melbourne, Russell and Rosemary Lucker of Karbeethong Lodge in Victoria and photographers Antoine Rozes and Jenny Wiedermann, Town & Country Collections in Melbourne, Hubert Baudoin and Thomas Gibson of The Moorings in the Florida Keys and Robyn Ross PR, Space Furniture, Mrs. Eugenie Voorhees of Nantucket and Mr Hugh Newell Jacobsen, Toby Tyler and Tracy Barry of The Landing on Harbour Island, The Raleigh hotel in Miami, The International in Brighton and designers Hecker Phelan Guthrie, JK Place in Florence, Uma Ubud in Bali, Designers Guild, 101 Hotel in Iceland, the Habita Monterrey hotel in Mexico and John Jacob Interiors in South Africa.